T0114975

Kioko

and the Legend of the Plains

 USHANGA BOOKS

First printed and published in Kenya in the Ushanga Book Series in 2015 by the Syokimau Cultural Centre, P.O Box 20257– 00100 Nairobi.

ISBN: 978—9966-7020-1-2

Series Editor: Emma Muli

For my mother, B. Ndulu Kyendo who told me this story when I was possibly a 10-year old boy.

CHAPTER ONE

CURIOSITY ABOUT THE LAND OF CATTLE

Kioko woke up to the sounds of chirping birds coming through the eaves of the house and the cock's loud crowing.

He adjusted the piece of cloth strapped across his shoulders and stepped out of the hut. The large purple and green bird that he loved was perched on the fence as it was every morning. Kioko stopped at a distance, admiring it.

"Can birds really talk?" he wondered as he always did. He wished he could catch the bird and hold it in his hands. It was so near - yet he knew it was not easy to catch. So many times he had tried to and so many times he had failed. Every time he tried, the bird would fly away and disappear into the thick, thorny bushes, its strong wings leaving a trail of sad sounds.

He was about to turn back to go into the house when his brother, Ndei, arrived with a catapult loaded with a stone. Before he could open his mouth to speak to Ndei, Kioko heard the swift sound of the stone as it flew past. The bird fell to the ground, kicking and turning in pain. Kioko ran to it, picked it up and, placing it on his palms, began blowing on it, hoping to revive it. It was too late. The bird stiffened and died.

Kioko cried and cried.

The boys in Kioko's small village of Nzaui laughed at him because of his unusual love for animals. Kioko especially loved big bulls with huge humps upon which he would ride home from the grazing fields.

His father was a famous warrior named Muendo. Every now and then, Muendo would lead a group of warriors on cattle raids. They would return with large herds of cattle.

There was always great rejoicing throughout the village of Nzaui and beyond when Muendo and the warriors returned. Bulls were slaughtered and there was much feasting. Children enjoyed such occasions greatly. But Kioko was sad at such moments because he hated to see animals slaughtered. It was even sadder for him when the animals killed were the bulls he loved so much.

One day, when his father and the warriors returned with another large herd of cattle, Kioko watched with tears in his eyes as the bull he had just trained to carry him was captured and tied with ropes, ready for slaughter. Overcome with emotions, Kioko ran to his father and begged him to spare the bull.

"Bulls are for eating! That is what they are kept for!" Muendo calmly rebuked his son. Then he pulled him aside. "Son," he said, " Son, you have got to be brave!"

Although he loved his son, Muendo feared that Kioko's love for animals would make him too weak to go out on cattle raids when he grew up. He often scolded him for not being as tough as other boys of his age.

Muendo had noticed that Kioko was rarely out fighting with other boys. He was also rarely out hunting lizards and birds with his small bow and arrows to prepare him for successful cattle raids.

What Muendo didn't know however, was that his son was, in truth, unlike other boys. For although he was only ten years old, Kioko was already yearning to go to the distant land from where the warriors went to get cattle and which the boys referred to as The Land of Cattle, He was yearning to go to bring his own big, fat bull — a bull that no one would kill.

It is very far, Grandmother said, "You walk and walk until your feet are as fat as those of an elephant..."

THAT evening he decided to find out more about the Land of Cattle.

"Tell me Grandmother, how far is the Land of Cattle?" Kioko asked.

"Very far," replied Grandmother. "It is very far," she repeated. "You walk and walk and walk until the sun sets and your feet swell so much until they become as fat as those of an elephant. And if you can still walk, you walk for many, many more days in the wilderness, where you fight with fierce lions, creeping, poisonous snakes and laughing hyenas... all kinds of fearsome animals! And if you are still alive, you reach Ukavi, the Land of Cattle."

Grandmother examined the boy's face through the dim light across the fireplace. She noticed Kioko was listening seriously. It frightened her.

"It is very, very far!" She added. Then she sighed. "Aha, we women don't know such things. I have never been to Ukavi!"

CHAPTER TWO

KIOKO'S SECRET STRENGTH

As Kioko herded cattle with other boys the next day, he thought only about the distant Land of Cattle which he now knew was called Ukavi. How far was it? What do the people who live there look like? What would they do to him if they caught him taking their bull? He wished that Grandmother knew more about these people who owned all the cattle.

He was still thinking about this when Ndava stood before him. Ndava was the big bully who always beat up small boys like Kioko. He was older and stronger than the other boys. Kioko, like the other small boys, feared and hated him. Today, Ndava was obviously out for a fight with Kioko.

Ndava drew a line on the dusty ground with his big toe. "You cross that line!" he dared Kioko in his usual proud manner. Kioko knew very well that was Ndava's way of starting fights. He ignored Ndava's clenched fist held before his eyes.

"Did you go to your father to beseech him not to kill a bull? Did you?" the bully mocked.

The boys had now formed a small crowd, waiting to witness the big

12

fight. Fighting was the most popular entertainment for them when they were in the fields herding cattle. Kioko wished the bully could just walk away. He didn't want to fight. He hated fights. Many times such fights left the boys bleeding badly, making their parents unhappy.

"You went to your father to beg him not to slaughter a bull, you silly, little cry-baby!" the bully repeated.

The other boys laughed. Tough boys, it was commonly known among the boys, didn't go crying to their fathers or mothers.

The bully pointed to the line on the ground again and said, "If you are not a cry baby, cross that line, now!"

Kioko examined the line but did not step over it. Instead, he fixed his angry eyes on his rival's, despising himself for allowing Ndava to bully him.

"I don't want to fight!" he said firmly.

"I don't want to fight" Ndava mimicked to the amusement of the boys. "So you don't want to fight? So you don't want to fight?"

Kioko was wondering how to get rid of the bully when, quick as lightning, Ndava's fist landed on his chin. His eyes went blind. He spat out blood. The boys laughed excitedly.

Suddenly, without thinking about what he was doing, Kioko hit Ndava hard on the forehead. Ndava fell to the ground. His nose was bleeding profusely. He quickly picked himself up, looked this way and that way, before fleeing at great speed. The boys laughed and jeered at the bully.

To the boys, Kioko had proved he was not a cry baby. He had proved he could fight. He had proved that he was a warrior. But to Kioko, it was this victory that made him sure he was now ready to go for a bull from Ukavi, the Land of Cattle.

CHAPTER THREE

JOURNEY BEGINS

That evening, Kioko thought about how he would travel to the Land of Cattle. Soon he got a plan. He would wait until the day his father and the warriors would be going for more cattle. He would follow them from a distance. This way he surely would reach the land of big, powerful bulls. In his mind's eye, he could already see himself riding on a huge bull with a huge hump which he had brought by himself from the Land of Cattle.

He didn't have long to wait, for soon he learnt that his father and the warriors were about to go on another cattle raid. Preparations started within a few days. New, strong bows and arrows were made. It was necessary to be well prepared because, as Grandmother had said, the journey to bring cattle from Ukavi was dangerous. The people who lived in Ukavi didn't like losing their cattle. He had also learned that many times there were big battles.

Kioko tested his bow and arrows. The journey to Ukavi was to start that evening. As usual, the elders and the priests had gathered to give advice and bless the warriors so that no harm would befall them.

When the warriors were ready to

depart, Kioko dashed to his Grandmother's house from where he planned to start his journey. Grandmother had just finished cooking. She gave him the large wooden cooking spoon which she had just used for him to scoop the remains of food with his finger.

Kioko saw the spoon was full of food. "How lucky!" he thought. "This will be my food on the journey!"

Stealthily, he crept to the bush where he had hidden his bow and arrows. From there, he could see when his father and the warriors were ready to start their journey.

"Go well and return with many, many healthy cattle! And may *Mulungu*, our creator, help you to return safely."

From where he was hiding, Kioko

could hear the cries of the children. They were sad to see their fathers go. Women also cried because they feared that their sons would not return.

With the help of the bright moon light, Kioko could see clearly as the warriors set out on their journey. It was time for him to follow.

He strapped his bow and arrows on his shoulders as he had seen the warriors do. *"Mulungu* help me to return with a healthy, beautiful and powerful bull. A bull with a huge hump. And may you *Mulungu* also help me return safely!" he prayed quietly for fear of being noticed.

Carefully, he followed the warriors, keeping close enough to see them and far enough not to be noticed.

It was a long journey from the hills of Nzaui to the plains. When the sun started to appear, Kioko and the warriors were already walking in deserted, endless plains with grass so tall that it almost covered him.

At midday, the warriors came upon a huge acacia tree that stood like an umbrella above the tall, green grass. Its branches spread out creating a perfect shade for the warriors.

The warriors sat down under the tree and started to take their food as they talked and laughed heartily. As Kioko watched from a distance, he felt pangs of hunger in his stomach. He took out the wooden spoon and tried to scoop some food from it. To his disappointment, the food had dried on the spoon. With his hands on his cheeks, he sat as he listened to the familiar song of a dove that now sounded sad.

It didn't take long before Kioko begun to nod with sleep for he was very tired and he had not slept the whole night. Soon he was fast asleep. In his sleep, he dreamed that he was falling from a tree. The impact of the fall was so great that it woke him up. He rubbed his eyes and looked around. Where was his father? Where were the warriors? To his bewilderment the warriors had disappeared. They had just vanished in the glittering mirages of the hot sun. Kioko held his breath and tried to listen. Everything was still and quiet.

The clear, blue sky was like one large void touching the earth at the distant horizon. Which way had the warriors followed? Kioko wondered, fear overcoming him. Which way was home? And which way was Ukavi?

These questions were crowding his mind when he suddenly felt something crawling up his legs. He jumped up and started running about to free himself from it. He was sure it was a snake. A large snake which would surely kill him. Grandmother had often told him that such snakes wound themselves round a persons body and crushed him with their powerful muscles.

He suddenly stopped jumping about and stood aside. He had noticed some movement in the grass. His heart was beating so fast and loud he could hear it. He carefully examined the place where he had been sitting. There was nothing that he could see. He tiptoed to his small luggage that consisted of a bow, arrows and the Grandmother's cooking spoon. He looked around. Then he saw a large lizard moving through the grass. He heaved a sigh of relief. There was no snake after all!

Loudly, he said to himself, "No, Kioko, you are not afraid. Now it's time to go. You're a tough man, who can beat Ndava, the bully." And with that he picked up his luggage and started running through the tall grass as he loudly sang a song he had made up to encourage himself.

Run, run, run, I will go with you

Run, run, run, to the Land of Cattle

Run, run, run to get a bull

Run, run to own and keep

Run, run, run and run.

His loud voice echoed in the distance, but there was no one to hear him, not even his father and the warriors whom he now wished could hear him.

CHAPTER FOUR

ALONE IN THE VAST PLAINS

In the plains, the sun was setting. Kioko suddenly felt cold and hungry. He had to find something to eat and a place to sleep. Sleeping on the ground was comfortable, he thought. But then he remembered the many dangerous creatures that lay hidden in the tall grass. What about sleeping on a tree? he wondered.

There were dangerous animals, of course, such as the leopards that loved sleeping on trees as Grandmother used to say. And there were snakes. Despite this, Kioko reasoned, danger was much less likely to occur on a tree than on the ground.

Soon he came upon a large baobab tree. It had a huge trunk and sprawling branches that crisscrossed to make a perfect bed. He took a few twigs, climbed the tree and spread the twigs on the branches to make a bed.

With the sleeping problem solved he set out to look for food. After he had unsuccessfully searched for berries, he took his bow and arrows and went to hunt birds. It was the first time that he had to kill a bird, and he kept praying that the unlucky bird would forgive him for killing it.

Soon he found a huge, flightless bird which he easily killed.

He lit a fire by rubbing two pieces of wood together like the boys in Nzaui always did when in the fields herding cattle. In a large piece of wood he made a hole. Out of the other wood, he made a spindle. Inserting the spindle into the hole, he incessantly rubbed it between his hands until it produced sparks of fire. He then added dry twigs and made a fire upon which he roasted the bird.

He made an opening in the stem of the baobab tree. And sure as Grandmother had told him, enough water for him to drink soon oozed out. and collected on the large leave he had place on the floor of the opening.

After eating, Kioko climbed up the tree to sleep. He had hardly closed his eyes when he heard the sounds of a galloping animal. Then he saw, with the help of the moonlight, a huge animal running at full speed towards the tree.

The animal suddenly stopped at the fire, its hind legs screeching on the ground and its forelegs lifted up to the air because of the speed. In great fury, it stomped on the fire until it was all put out. Kioko stayed still, firmly holding onto the tree. He knew that a simple mistake could cost him his life. He was relieved when the buffalo went away after putting off the fire.

Although the buffalo didn't harm him, Kioko was too scared to sleep. But he was also too tired to stay awake. Soon sleep overcame him.

And the sleep was so deep that he didn't even know when he fell down from the tree. He just continued sleeping on the ground.

He was awakened by sounds of scratching on the ground. He rubbed his eyes only to stare at the blazing eyes of a lion barely a few feet away from him. He stared at the lion and the lion stared back. Kioko couldn't believe that there, before him, stood the most dangerous animal staring at him.

In one quick move, the lion's large paw will strike and I will be gone, Kioko thought. Then he remembered what Grandmother had told him: "Do not move, just stay still and the animal will move on. Animals never attack people unless they are provoked." And that was the only weapon he had right now. "Please

Mulungu help me this time, and I will go home! I want to go home, please help me!" he prayed silently.

For what looked like a very long time to Kioko, the lion watched him and he continued praying to *Mulungu* for help while staring back at the fierce animal, his breath held back, his body stiff and still.

He was relieved when the lion relaxed its stare and moved away. Its slow, majestic walk was so reassuring that Kioko's fear quickly turned into admiration. If only he had stretched his arm to touch it!

He watched the lion as it went past a large herd of wildebeest which got frightened and scampered in all directions. But the lion wasn't concerned with them. It just went ahead without hurrying, as if it

When he woke up, he stared into the fiery eyes of a lion.

didn't have a care in the world. Suddenly it stopped and looked back at Kioko before it turned away and disappeared into the tall grass.

CHAPTER FIVE

DESPERATE SEARCH FOR KIOKO IN NZAUI

Back in the village of Nzaui, Kioko's mother Mutile had noticed that her son was missing only when the family was going to sleep. Since then she had searched everywhere in the village but she had not found the boy. "I gave him the spoon to clean and he did not return," said Grandmother who was among the search party.

"When were you with him?"

asked Kioko's uncle who was also Grandmother's last born son. Uncle, whom the children called Mwendwau, was still too young to accompany the warriors to the Land of Cattle.

"Just before the warriors left," said Grandmother. Then she remembered that she had heard the boy asking curious questions about Ukavi. "Might the boy have decided to go there? Can he have followed his father?"

"To where?" Mutile asked.

"To Ukavi. I heard him ask many questions about Ukavi. When I gave him the spoon to clean, I noticed he was restless. I didn't think much about it."

"But a young boy like that... it is impossible! He wouldn't do such a thing!" said Mwendwau. "The boy must be just around."

"Around where?" asked Mutile, helplessly. "We have searched everywhere. We've asked everyone we know. Just where could he be?"

Mwendwau cupped his hands to form the shape of a trumpet around his mouth and called out, "K - i - o - k - o!!!" His voice echoed in the stillness of the night but there was no answer.

Silently, Mwendwau and the two women started on their way back home, each full of fearful thoughts.

Back home, Kioko was still nowhere to be seen.

"My son is dead! He is dead!" Mutile cried out, now unable to control her tears.

"He's not dead! He will come back," Grandmother comforted her, but Mutile had already disappeared into her room, crying uncontrollably.

"I know I'll never see him again. I know he will never come back!" she cried.

CHAPTER SIX

THE RETURN OF THE LION

The sun stood overhead in the wilderness on yet another day since Kioko and the warriors left home. He had been sitting under an acacia tree since sunrise wondering which direction to follow. He thought about home. Which way was home? In the plains, there was no way to know.

Only tall grass calmly swayed in the burning sun. The only familiar thing was the sad song of a dove:

Dudu, du du du du

The child, what's it suffering from?

It's suffering from chronic cough

Spit on it so it is cured

Dudu, du du du du

The dove's song reminded Kioko of a story Grandmother had told him about a weak and helpless woman who sent a bird to her husband. The woman had just given birth and was being mistreated by an *aimu* — a cheeky ogre who ate all her food. The husband was working far away as a blacksmith and when the bird gave him the message, he came home swiftly to rescue her.

Suddenly it occurred to Kioko that may be he, too, could send the dove home just like the blacksmith's wife sent the bird to her husband. Turning over Grandmother's story in his head, Kioko became so engrossed in it that he begun to imagine himself talking with the dove the same way the blacksmith's wife did.

"You, dove on the tree, what would you ask for if I sent you to Grandmother in Nzaui." And the dove said, "Give me some fruits from that tree."

Kioko gave the dove the fruits, and off it went. It flew so swiftly that it soon perched on the big *muumo* tree next to the stone where Grandmother was winnowing her millet.

The dutiful dove started to sing its message:

You Grandmother winnowing her

millet

Your Grandson is lost in the plains
His food is wild animals and fruits.

In his mind's eye, Kioko saw Grandmother listening carefully. Then she said to his mother, Mutile "I think there is a message the bird is telling me. Let me listen!" Then she knew for sure it was a message about Kioko who is lost in the plains.

He saw Grandmother call strong young men to follow the bird. They soon arrived and carried Kioko high on their shoulders to his Grandmother...

The silence of the dove awoke Kioko from his day dream. Now, here he was in the vast plains without directions. How was he going to reach home again? He didn't know how far he had walked. He just didn't know anything anymore. He had never felt so hungry, thirsty, tired and lonely. And on top of it all, he was fearful.

He was afraid of the many frightening things that lay in the plains which Grandmother used to tell him about. He tried to force them out of his mind, but one story kept forcing itself in. It was about the dreadful giants who lived in the plains.

Grandmother had told him of her frightening encounter with one of them when she was a small girl living in the plains with her family. Water was scarce, so Grandmother and other girls used to wake up before the first cock crow, so that they could reach the river before others arrived and scooped the river bed dry.

At the huge dry riverbed, the girls would dig up small wells. Then they would wait for the water to seep slowly through the sand and collect in the small wells they had made.

One early morning, as they waited for their small wells to fill, the girls saw, right there in front of them, a giant. The giant was so tall that his head disappeared into the sky. The girls tried to run back home, but the giant was there in front of them. Then they tried to run across the river. And the giant was there again in front of them. Whichever way they ran, the giant was there - in front of them! Overwhelmed, the girls collapsed.

Kioko shut his eyes tightly to keep

out the frightening memory. Thinking of it had made him so afraid that he could imagine the giant standing there in front of him. He quickly picked up his luggage and continued his journey, singing and skipping to keep away the frightening memories:

Run, run, run, I will go with you

Run, run, run to the Land of Cattle

Run, run, run to get a bull

Run, run, run to own and keep

Run, run, run and run.

The sight of a beautiful baby rabbit interrupted his singing and skipping. He tiptoed to the small bush where the animal had disappeared into hoping to catch it. He searched the surrounding bushes but there was no rabbit in sight.

He was about to turn away when he heard the sound of an animal scratching on the ground. He turned to look. To his amazement, it was the lion that he had seen before, its flaming eyes fixed on him. It stood, barely an arm's-length away from him. Frightened, he stood still and stared at it - his eyes fixed on those of the animal. He dared not show his fear to the animal.

But soon, fear overwhelmed him. "Now I am surely going to be killed by this animal, " he told himself. "No one is here to save me! No one will ever know what happened to me!" Then he started to cry, calling on his Grandmother to help him.

The lion softened its stare. And Kioko watched it walk away slowly and majestically.

It walked towards a pool where a large number of animals collected, apparently enjoying the evening sun. It roared, its thunderous sound filling the earth. The animals quickly scattered, leaving the pool empty.

The lion turned and stared at Kioko. Driven by a huge thirst, Kioko thought he saw the lion beckoning him to the pool. He examined the lion uncertainly. He saw it walk a short distance away from the pool. Then it stood looking at Kioko. To Kioko, it seemed as if its eyes were pleading, as if it was inviting him to take some water.

Kioko took a few, careful steps towards the pool, all the time watching the lion. Even if he tried to run away, he reasoned, he would never outpace this animal. And with that reasoning, he rushed to the pool and scooped some water with his hands.

When he had drank enough, he turned and looked at the lion, which still stood in the same place watching him. Its fierce eyes now seemed friendly to Kioko. The lion then started to walk away. Kioko watched it until it disappeared into the tall grass.

Picking his way through the tall grass, Kioko wished the lion could speak. If it could just speak and tell him where he was! Or if it could be just like his bulls — friendly and obedient. Then he would climb onto it, and with its great speed, he would surely find his way home.

The lion stood a short distance away as Kioko drank the water.

He was coming to a place that looked like a clearing with short grass when he suddenly noticed the lion again. It stood there, in front of him, with a small antelope held between its teeth. Kioko's heart began beating fast.

Although it had not attacked him, Kioko didn't know when the lion would set upon him. He stared at the lion which stared back at him with its fierce but friendly eyes. The lion put down the carcass and moved a short distance away. It stopped, folded its feet and lay on the grass.

Kioko picked up the carcass, and using his pieces of wood, he lit a fire. He had started to roast his meat when he saw a buffalo running towards him at great speed. Without thinking, he fled towards the lion and collapsed on its huge body. The lion, which had apparently gone into a nap, stirred and roared, sending the buffalo fleeing away from the fire. Surprisingly, the lion didn't hurt Kioko. Instead, it returned to its position and continued its nap as Kioko went back to continue roasting his meat.

After eating, Kioko continued on his journey. He walked past a group of tall, long-necked giraffes that made him feel so small. Then he walked past wildebeests and antelopes. He stopped to watch a herd of elephants. Grandmother had told him that elephants are so huge that as girls, they used to swim in the pools made by their hooves.

He was still wondering about the size of the elephant's feet when he saw a warthog running at great speed towards him. Grandmother had told him that   warthogs cut people's heads.

"The way to stop a warthog killing you," Grandmother had instructed, "is to put a basket on your head. It picks only what is on top. But you have to stay still or else you will lose your head!"

Kioko did not have a basket, so he put his bows and arrows on his head, closed his eyes and waited for the worst to happen. After what seemed a long time, he opened his eyes, only to see the lion's bright eyes staring at him. He couldn't help smiling at the lion with joy, but the animal's face remained blank, but friendly as it walked away.

CHAPTER SEVEN

AMAZING SCENES

IT was on a bright moonlit night when Kioko suddenly heard the mooing of cattle. Carefully, he listened. And just when he was about to run towards the direction of the sounds, fear overcame him. Maybe he was in the land of the frightening, invisible spirits that Grandmother had told him about.

"They do their things like people. Only they work when people are asleep," Grandmother said. "You can hear them passing by in the cattle tracks driving their cattle home. The cattle moo and bellow. You can even hear the clink, clunk of the bells on their necks."

He was torn between fear and the desire to get help to reach home. Then an idea came to him: No matter who they were, he would try to talk to them. Maybe they could listen to him and help him get home He suddenly felt confident as if he was standing in daylight with many people beside him. He moved forward quickly.

To his surprise, he came upon a most amazing sight. There, before his eyes, stood the largest herd of cattle that he had ever seen. And just next to him, the bull he had always dreamed of owning stood, staring at

The cattle followed raising great dust that was visible from far away.

him. Only a weak fence of dry tree branches stood between him and the bull.

It was healthy, big and strong with a huge hump. In the moonlight he could see its bright eyes fixed on him. Kioko tiptoed to the entrance of the cattle enclosure. Behind the bull the rest of the cattle calmly slept. He surveyed the place and listened carefully. There was no noise at all. It seemed as if everyone was already fast asleep. Carefully, he opened the enclosure and walked to the bull.

Softly, he stroked the bull's back, feeling the smoothness of its fur. He spread out his hand and he felt the warm, rough tongue of the bull pass over it. To Kioko, the licking of his hand was a sign that the bull was friendly. He climbed onto the bull and it started off at great speed facing the direction he thought was home. In his mind, there was only one wish - to reach home and see his Grandmother again.

In the moonlight, he could see they were travelling through the same plains he had passed earlier on his way. He could see the lone acacia trees standing like lonely sentinels in the vast plains. And he hoped he was on his way home where he would fall into the arms of Grandmother. "Grandmother will give me sour porridge from her special gourd," Kioko thought "She will be so happy to see me. And she will be so proud of me."

The thought of seeing Grandmother again spurred him on and he increased speed as he sung:

It is my bull, I say it is

I raided it with a tiny flame, I say I did

A tiny bow of muvau *tree, I say it is*

And tiny arrows of mutili, *I say they are*

As he sung the bull, bellowed and bellowed. Soon it was morning. With the daylight he could now clearly see the familiar places where he had passed through in the plains.

When he reached the huge baobab tree where he had met the friendly lion, Kioko stopped and climbed down from the bull, hoping to see the lion. Then he climbed the tree hoping he could see the hills of Nzaui. What caught his eyes however, was the amount of cattle that were following him. They were so many he couldn't count them.

Another thing caught his eyes also - a big cloud of dust that twirled to the skies. It was clear the Akavi were following him, just like Grandmother had told him they would.

He decided to flee on the bull. Maybe he would reach home before the Akavi caught up with him. By the time the bull started, the cattle had caught up, raising great dust that was visible from far away.

Frantically, Kioko kicked the bull's sides with his feet to nudge it to pick greater speed. But the bull could only move at that much speed. Suddenly, in front of him he saw them - the strong Akavi men with long red hair, just like Grandmother had described them. Their long sharp spears were flying in the air, ready to strike.

Trapped, Kioko stood transfixed atop the bull. He watched with increasing anxiety as the Akavi warriors searched all over the place for something which he couldn't understand.

Thoughts of Grandmother came flooding into his mind. She had warned him and he had not listened. Now he would never see her again. *Never again!* He heard himself say as tears flooded his eyes and he let them flow down his face, crying like the small baby he was.

When they had completed their search, the warriors gathered around him and talked animatedly for some time. Then they apparently agreed on a plan because some of them started rounding the cattle and driving them back. They didn't spear him as he had expected they would. They didn't even remove him from the bull's back. Instead they let him ride on.

"I should run away," he thought. But there were so many warriors armed with sharp spears that the thought of fleeing disappeared immediately. It was clear he could not outrun these people. What would they do to him? He wondered. Were they planning to kill him in their village?

When they arrived at the village, many people, including children, were outside to watch the warriors return. There were many boys some of whom stood with their mouths wide open, their arms clasped at the back of their heads as if to support their huge heads. "They look just like the boys at home in Nzaui," Kioko thought.

One of the warriors came over to Kioko and helped him to come off the bull. Were these people friendly or was this what they did before they killed someone? Kioko wondered. He was wondering thus when another warrior brought him a gourd full of milk. He made a sign for him to drink the milk. These were certainly not the Akavi that Grandmother talked about!

In the night, they took him to an open place where they roasted meat on a big fire and ate directly from the fire as they talked and laughed heartily. Each person had a long knife with which he sliced off huge chunks of meat. Women and children frequently came in and out of the houses to get chunks of roasted meat. Kioko was served his meat cut into smaller pieces. Everyone seemed so happy that Kioko actually forgot about his predicament and found himself laughing with the people although he didn't understand what they were talking about.

He ate to his satisfaction. "These must be very good people," Kioko thought to himself. "Here I was fleeing with their cattle, and yet they are treating me so kindly. Of course, they will kill me in the end!" Kioko's mind could not stop turning things over.

When it was time to sleep, he lay on the floor on a cowhide like the rest of the children. Kioko took long to sleep, trying to listen in case he was in danger.

As he lay down to sleep, many thoughts passed through his mind. He wished he could speak the Akavi language. He would make these men with long, braided red hair know he was an innocent boy coming only for a bull. He would make them know that he didn't want all the cattle that followed him. And that all he wanted was a bull. A strong, healthy bull to ride upon.

Then he could tell them about Grandmother - how he loved her and how he missed her. Grandmother must be missing him too. O yes, he could tell them about his mother and his warrior father. No, he wouldn't tell them about his father. They would surely kill him if he did.

With these thoughts running in his mind, he soon fell asleep. He was woken up in the morning by the voice of a woman offering him a gourd of milk.

During the day, only women and small children were left in the village. Kioko was kept inside a house and his food was brought in by the women.

******

One afternoon, he was very hungry because the women had not brought him food. He was so desperate that when a woman brought him a gourd of milk, he almost snatched it from her. She handed him the gourd and walked out leaving some small boys behind.

Kioko held the gourd firmly in his hands, but before he could drink the milk a naughty boy snatched it and dashed out of the house with it. After a while, the woman returned with a bowl of meat. She was a friendly woman because when she put the food on the floor for Kioko to pick, she smiled warmly at him before she left. But no sooner had she left the room than the naughty boy again entered and snatched the food. Kioko was so desperate and infuriated that he kicked and punched the boy.

The boy ran out wailing. He soon returned with a bunch of bigger boys armed with clubs, ready to punish Kioko. As one of the boys lifted his club ready to strike, there was a sudden loud roar of a lion that deafened the ears. The boys scattered fleeing in different directions as women rushed to the scene to see what had happened. Confused by the events, Kioko stood still, his heart beating so loud he could hear it.

That evening a large crowd gathered to see the "lion boy." Word had spread all over the village that the little boy who had tried to take away the cattle was not human but a lion.

A man who was clothed in a lion's skin pushed forward through the crowd towards Kioko. He stood next to Kioko and studied his face for a long time, before he asked him in the language of the people of Nzaui what his name was.

"Kioko," the boy answered. "Kioko

son of Muendo!"

The man again studied the boy's face for a long time, but said nothing. What was he thinking about? Kioko wondered. Then he thought: Maybe I should not have mentioned the name of my warrior father. Maybe these people know him, and now they will surely kill me.

CHAPTER EIGHT

FEAR AND SADNESS IN THE VILLAGE OF NZAUI

It was noon of a hot day when the Nzaui warriors, led by Kioko's father, Muendo, arrived back home, tired and disappointed. They had reached Ukavi, the Land of Cattle, and had waited until it was very dark and safe to raid the cattle. But when they had opened the gate of the cattle enclosure where their spy had seen many fat cows and bulls, the cattle had made a lot of noise, waking up the Akavi warriors who soon overpowered them.

The whole village of Nzaui came to receive the warriors, anxious to know whether they had brought Kioko back with them.

"He disappeared the same day you left," Mutile told her husband, explaining to him what Grandmother had said.

"If he followed us, there's very little chance we will find him. He must have been killed by wild animals or died of hunger and thirst in the plains," Muendo said.

"Don't talk like that," Grandmother admonished. "That boy is courageous. He will come back. He will return!"

"But it's now so many days," Mutile said. "He must be dead by now."

Grandmother put her comforting arm around Mutile's shoulder. "Don't wish that on your child. The boy will return!"

The news that the warriors had not seen Kioko brought fresh gloom upon the village of Nzaui. People spoke about the missing boy in hushed tones and whispers. It was a matter of days, they believed, and they would get the sad news. Perhaps a stranger would come from another village asking if anyone had lost a son.

Then they would tell him that they had, indeed, lost a small boy. The stranger would then tell them of a boy with a bow, arrows and a wooden cooking spoon who was found dead in the bush. Then they would know it was Kioko, the ten year old boy who went on a cattle raid in the Land of Cattle, alone.

CHAPTER NINE

PLEASANT SURPRISE

Meanwhile in Ukavi many bulls were slaughtered for a great celebration. There was a huge gathering at the largest acacia tree in the center of the village. The man dressed in the lion skin sat in the middle of the crowd. After the feast, two young but strong warriors led Kioko to the middle of the crowd where the man with the lion skin sat.

This was the moment that Kioko

feared. Grandmother had warned him that the Akavi were not happy to lose their cattle. In his mind's eye, he could already see the huge crowd tearing him apart.

He could see them laughing and cheering as they tore him apart. After that they will probably forget him like he never existed. They will forget him the way the people of Nzaui forget the bulls they slaughter.

Kioko tried to keep his mind away from these frightening thoughts. Instead, he encouraged himself by remembering that he could tell his story to the man with the lion skin who would surely understand.

He would tell him that all he wanted was a bull - a big bull with a huge hump which he could ride on. He would tell him that he had not come to take their cattle. He would tell him that he didn't want all the cattle that followed him. Surely he would listen to him. When Kioko was seated, the crowd went quiet as if expecting a great announcement. The man dressed in lion skin started speaking and spoke for a long time, with the crowd often clapping their hands, sometimes laughing heartily or ululating in agreement.

He cut into Kioko's thoughts when he motioned him to move closer. He put his hand on the boy's head saying something that made everyone laugh and stomp their feet.

Then speaking in the language of the people of Nzaui, the man falteringly told Kioko that within a few days, he and the warriors would take him back home to Nzaui.

CHAPTER TEN

THE REUNION

One afternoon, in Nzaui village, as Mutile and Grandmother winnowed their millet on the flat rock in the fields, Grandmother suddenly paused.

"Do you hear the voice of someone? I can hear the voice of a boy. It sounds like Kioko's!"

Mutile tried to listen but she heard nothing.

"The boy must be dead by now. It has been many days since he disappeared," she said. Mutile had received so many false stories about the return of her son that she had grown weary.

"No," insisted Grandmother, putting her hand behind her ear so that she could catch the sound better. "I hear the voice of a boy singing. Listen!"

The two women listened keenly. Mutile could now hear the faint voice of a boy. The voice drew nearer and nearer, so that the women could make out that it was, indeed, the voice of Kioko. They could clearly hear the song Kioko was singing:

It is my bull, I say it is

I got it from the Land of Cattle, I say I did

My uncle gave it to me, I say he did

And with Akavi warriors he led us home, I say he did.

As Kioko drew nearer the village of Nzaui, the bull bellowed and bellowed. The whole village came out to watch. Kioko was riding on top of the big bull with a huge hump. And behind him was a group of young men with long red hair that the people of Nzaui knew were Akavi warriors. They were driving the largest, healthiest herd of cattle ever seen in the village.

Kioko, the cattle and the Akavi warriors rounded the village of Nzaui several times as he sang and the bull bellowed. The villagers watched in amazement. It was a spectacle that they had never seen before.

Grandmother and Mutile arrived at the homestead at the same time that Kioko and his group also arrived. It was as if the man who wore a lion skin had been struck by thunderbolt at the sight of Grandmother. He rushed to her and grabbed her, holding her close to his chest. "Oh mama, Oh, mama!" was all he could say.

Grandmother was overcome with emotion. "My son! Kioko, my long lost son!" she said repeatedly.

Even though it had been many, many years since he was abducted as a small boy during a cattle raid, Grandmother could recognize her

It was as if Ole Lavi was struck by a thunderbolt when he saw his mother. They recognized each other immediately.

son at once.

Muendo, Kioko's father, came running when he heard that his long lost brother had returned.

"My brother! My dear brother!" he hugged his elder brother, tears of joy falling on his face.

When his brother was abducted as a small boy, Muendo, like the rest of the family, had hoped that he would manage to escape and return to Nzaui. They had hoped and prayed. As years went by however, their hopes had waned and eventually the family had despaired.

Suddenly. a warrior of the Akavi sprung up from the crowd, his long braids flying in the air. He cried aloud with joy as he had recognized his sister who had been abducted as a small girl by the Nzaui warriors.

Tears flowed freely as brother and sister embraced. To everyone it was an unforgettable emotional moment.

******

In the days following the arrival of the Akavi warriors in Nzaui, Ole Lavi, for that was the Ukavi name of the man dressed in lion skin - showed the warriors the places of his childhood. He showed them the grazing fields, the millet farms and the rivers from which the cattle drank. He showed them the paths through which he rode his bulls.

During their stay, more people reunited with their long lost relatives. It was also during those days that Kioko learned that he was named after Ole Lavi and that Ole Lavi, too, loved animals, especially bulls.

Muendo explained how he had been bitter when his brother was abducted and how he had decided to name his son Kioko to preserve the memories of his brother.

And Ole Lavi, showed them the family ornaments which he had preserved throughout the years. He told them that he wore the lion skin to commemorate his Nzaui clan totem which was a lion.

CHAPTER ELEVEN

NEW DAWN

Days quickly went by. It was time for Ole Lavi whose Nzaui name was Kioko, and the Akavi warriors to return home. The village of Nzaui put up the largest feast ever in their honor.

On the evening of the feast everyone in the village turned up at the giant muumo tree. They all came splendid in their ceremonial attire. There was heavy drumming, dancing and feasting. Even the little children were out at the muumo tree dancing to the rhythm of drums. When Muendo stood up, the drumming and dancing abruptly stopped. Then he started to speak.

"My people of Nzaui: We are gathered here to honour our dear brothers from Ukavi."

He called out the name of Kioko and both Kioko his brother from Ukavi and Kioko his son, came forward from the crowd and stood next to him.

"My people of Nzaui: Until now, the people of Ukavi have been a people who only raid our cattle and take our children and women away. People who were faceless and despicable.

"It has always been like that. It was like that for our great, great grandfathers. It was like that for our grandfathers. It was like that for our fathers. It was like that for us, too."

Muendo paused. The crowd was silent.

"To me, however, it was not just tradition. It was not just a cattle raid. It was revenge. When the Akavi raided us and took away my brother, Kioko, who now stands here beside me, I swore to myself and all those who knew me, that I would never rest until I avenged him. It became my life – bitterness and revenge."

He paused.

"You all know how sad I was when I thought my son here would not be strong enough to carry on the revenge. I was heartbroken. I was disappointed. I was frustrated!"

Muendo paused again to regain his self-control. He feared that the tears welling up in his eyes would start to flow. "Little did I know that the brother I was fighting for, the brother I wished to avenge, was the same brother I was going to hurt!

"But my son here - my son has brought new light to me. He has brought to us the faces of the people who live in Ukavi, the distant Land of Cattle..."

Muendo could no longer hold his tears. Ole Lavi put his strong arms around his brother and the young Kioko. And for a long time they embraced as tears freely flowed over their faces.

Ole Lavi started to speak.

"My people of Nzaui... When I saw this small boy I instantly saw myself in him... And when he told me his name, I knew my desire, ...my greatest desire ..was being fulfilled..." He could not continue as tears blinded his eyes and his voice chocked.

Kioko moved forward. He wanted to speak for his uncle, no, for his father but he could not speak. He could only hear his voice singing:

It is my bull, I say it is

I got it from the Land of Cattle, I say I did

My uncle gave it to me, I say he did

And, with Akavi warriors he led us home, I say he did.

The bull bellowed and bellowed and the lion roared and roared. The people embraced, weeping for the joy that Kioko had brought them. In the crowd no one could tell the villagers of Nzaui from the warriors of Ukavi.

Grandmother stood in the center studying the moon above. It was so clear! To her it was a heavenly sign of peace and harmony. She closed her eyes and envisioned the future of her children - the people of Nzaui and the people of Ukavi.

In her mind she could see the two faces of her children - and they were both smiling.

Printed in the United States
By Bookmasters